HEARTBEATS

A JOURNEY THROUGH THE SOUL

By

Ronette D. Jacobs

Ronette D. Jacobs

Library of Congress Cataloging-in-Publication Data

ISBN-13: 978-1490980324
ISBN-10: 1490980326

DEDICATION

This book is dedicated to God from whom all of my help has come!

Table of Contents

ACKNOWLEDGMENTS

Thank you to my mother, Frances A. Sanderlin, who is my greatest cheerleader! Thanks for your constant and fervent prayers that help propel and sustain me to see this dream fulfilled.

Thank you to my godchildren: Amani, Anthronique, Kayla, Keeley, Jamie, Latané, and Ricky, Jr. Each of you has been the wind beneath my wings! Your love has been the force to carry me along to the completion of this project.

Thank you to my family, friends, "sons", and "daughters" who have been my greatest encouragers through the years to help flame the fire!

Thank you to my angelic daughters: Alexandria, Amani, Ashley, Brianna, Jcelyn, and Lindsay, who have been my life's greatest joys! Thank you for the constant push to keep writing!

Also, I thank Dr. Angela Corprew-Boyd who provided her editorial expertise and summative review. Thanks for your support and "iron sharpens iron" philosophy.

Thank you to Linda Mose Meadows for her aesthetic review, editorial assistance, advice, faith, and encouragement. You are a true trailblazer!

Thank you to Amani Morrison for her aesthetic reviews and editorial assistance. You have been my champion!

Thank you to James Jenkins for your technical assistance. You were a true lifesaver!

Finally, I thank my prayer partners Lucille Christie, Rev. Trina Jones, Shannon Thorne-Brackett, and Cheryl Walker who have continued to press in with me and for me through the years. Thank you all so much. Your prayers have been my sustaining strength.

To My Welcomed Readers:

The poems in this book were written as in invitation to cause us to pause and reflect on our very own life journey. It is through my soul that these poems were formed, lived, breathed, experienced, and observed. It is through my journey in life and intersections with others, both spiritual and natural, that each of these words became life. It is my hope that you will pick up this book at the right time in your life and that it will be an inspiration to you to take your own journey through your soul to find life's greatest Satisfier!

Humbly,
Ronette

Synapse

A moment…a time …a second…a year…a moment
An unexplainable place
A place, which demands patience
A time requiring silence and stillness
The unshakeable moment
Time to see clearly
Time to reflect
Time to be real
From a moment…a second…a year…a moment in between
Words cannot measure this moment
Unveiling of the heart and its real revelations
An unmasking of the expectations and
perilous weights placed upon
No need for explanation
Trash the calendar
Trash the old way
Trash the hustle and bustle
Release yesterday and embrace tomorrow
An unfolding of what has been there all along
A release to truth
No return to the past
No return to regrets
No need for permanency
No need to respond to others' questions
No return to dead moments and dead things
A birthing of something new yet to unfold
An in between place

Ronette D. Jacobs

Dreamkillers

For as long as I can remember, dreamkillers
have always swarmed around me.
Days and weeks and sometimes months would come,
and I would leap forward.
But out of nowhere came those dreamkillers
who swarmed around me.

One of them lingered over me
telling me day by day
That the next day I could start on my dream.
From day to day and year to year,
my dreams sat aimlessly by.
A glimmer of my dream over here,
a glimmer of my dream over there---
I will get to it is what the dreamkiller promised me
Until I shot procrastination dead in the face.

Another one came that kept me
lying around longer than I should have.
One hour turned to two and then to three and sometimes four.
What happened to my day I would ask?
The dreamkiller told me tomorrow would be better.
As the hours crept by so did the weeks
and then the months and soon the years.
All of which had been slept away.
Laziness had to be thrown in a can and set on fire.

Yet another one came. Fine as a crystal glass,
full of charisma, but loaded with deceit.
Promising the world, yet killing my dreams.
Offering me gold and handing me gold-plated.
Professing to know God but living like a heathen.
Offering a life filled with love but
incapable of moving beyond self.
This dreamkiller, called man, had to be erased.

From within rose up another dreamkiller,
one that professed the *I can'ts*.
This killer offered every scenario of how
things would not and could not work.
For every dream, there was a stream of *no's*.
For every sunshine, self brought along a cloud.
Self still tried to eliminate the future.
Self – the old self- the old mind-
had to be killed once and for all.

Hence, a final gathering and funeral were
held for all dreamkillers.
The grave was swiftly opened.
The casket was deeply lowered.
The dirt was adamantly tossed.
Dreamkillers:: dead and buried never to be resurrected!

Ronette D. Jacobs

Obligation

To be true to yourself
To be sincere in motives
To honor the office

To surrender to the real you
To be honest with others and yourself
To laugh at yourself daily

To give up the slips and dips
To move forward
To die fulfilled

To become empowered
To enjoy cotton candy
To love your work

To love your man
To love your woman
To love your child

To live beyond your circle
To serve others selflessly
To hold onto nothing or no one too tightly

To enjoy your childhood
To hold a newborn baby
To converse with an elderly wise person

To love yourself
To step out of the boat
To fulfill the desires of your heart

To make time for people who matter
To make time for things that make a difference
To make time to examine your soul's journey

My Friend

I didn't know that the day I last saw you would be the last day.
I had hoped that this day would have never come, but it has.
How is it that you, being in my life in every way,
Are not there at all anymore?

I didn't know the day would come so soon when I would not
hear your voice again.
Your laugh helped ease the pain of a stressful day at work.
Seeing your name show up as my phone rang made my heart
leap for joy.
You not being here is more painful than I could have imagined.

I didn't know that day we last shared a meal together would be
our last time.
Oh, how I miss sharing a bowl of warm apple cobbler and ice
cream with you.
We faced the challenges of life and the loss of things dear and
true.
You were there. My sunshine you became. My strength you
became. My iron you were.

I didn't know that the last time I saw you would be the last.
For if I had known, I would have told you that I loved you
longer.
For if I had known, I would have really told you how much your
prayers meant to me.
For if I had known, I would have made you laugh until your
stomach ached.
For if I had known, I would not have taken your mercy for
granted so much.
For if I had known, I would have looked beyond my pressures of
life to see that you, too, needed a friend...

Oh, how I miss you.

Ronette D. Jacobs

Daughter

If I had one moment with you,
what would I say?
If I could but just hold you tight
and shield you from this world of thorns, and
If I had to carry you in my bosom, I would.

You see, you mean the world to me
though we have never met.
You see, I have spent my whole life
wanting to be the best mother I could be for you.
Yet, we have never met.

The gentleness of your skin
and the glistening of your brown eyes
Yet, we have never met.
To hear you once say, "Mom"
and for my heart to answer "yes"
To grab hold of your hand
to keep you from crossing the wrong streets

To lead you to the living waters
where you would never die of thirst
Yet, we have never met.
If I had one day to see you
If I had one day to hold you
If I had one day to let you know

For I see you brown and beautiful
For I see you happy as a baby bird
discovering its first tiny worm
For I see you tumbling
around discovering new wonders

I see you baby girl,
Beautiful and bright

Pretty and precious
Giggly and gorgeous

I see you baby girl
reaching out for me.
I am here;
just come a little further.
For I have always been here.

Just for you.

What Will It Be?

Idea
Conception
Process
Plan
Birth
What Will It Be?

Labor pains
Morning
Noon
Night
No sleep
No rest
What Will It Be?

Anxiety
Contacts
Appointments
Fear
Stumbles
Jumping
What Will It Be?

Growing pains
A connection of souls
A sparkle of materialization
A fragment of reality
Knowledge of existence
Unable to see
What Will It Be?

A dream
For a long time
A hope
For a real time
A desire
For an increasing time

A manifestation
For a true time

It will be…the dream I dreamt.
It will be…that thing for which I had I hoped.
It will be…the one that brings happiness to my soul.

My heart's desire.

Ronette D. Jacobs

Coming Home

Having sat in that desert now for some odd months
What has changed?
Is it her walk?
Or is it her talk?
What about her sweet smile with that one little crooked tooth
On the right side of her mouth?

Oh, will she still smell innocent?
Oh, it has been such a long time.
Time---oh, what has time done now?
Will she still want to sit on my lap?

Will she still know it is me by the turn of my key?
Have the moments away stolen my space?
I love her so…she has her mother's eyes and my big hands.
Oh, I dread coming home and not knowing if she still knows me.

Will she still want the Barbie or is that doll now an old name?
My heart hates being so far away from home…
My soul hates the unknown…

Oh, how I love my country!
Oh, how I love my girl…growing so fast…
My heart aches to see her.
Oh, how I wish that coming home was a certainty.
Oh, how I wish that I could be in two places.

Coming home…may the chokehold of fear disappear
into a deep fog.
May I be overtaken by love and hugs and familiarity.
May I be overtaken by smells of innocence and warm
welcoming smiles.

Coming home…
May my heart be able to contain her smile again.

Rain

Earthly

Morning dew---
A rhythmic flow from the clouds
Yet, none the same

Heaping upon the blades of green growing grass
Each drop giving a refreshing moment to the earth
Washing away the soiled and renewing the old

Heavenly

When the soul is dry and thirsty…
When a desert land and the valley are one's resting places
Oh, how the rains from heaven fulfill deep thirsts

Tenderness fills the rough places again
A cup overflows…from bitterness to love
Rain…comes to bring new life…a new beginning

Rain
Drops
Refreshing
Cleansing
Pure

A dry land
An empty place
Crack, crevice, and crumbled…dry
A barren land

Waiting…
Just for the rain
Waiting…
Just for the rain

Then, a rain
Comes to overflow
To satisfy
To inspire new breaths

From Afar

Had it been somewhere
...I would have never noticed
But I did see it, truly
It looked so real.
Too real
But could it be...a star...an illusion?

No, it was the dream...the one.
He came in tenderly.
Never rushing, pushing, or shoving
Never boasting about who He was
Or what He was going to do
But, gently He came in.

With Him, He brought hope.
With Him, He brought love.
With Him, He brought peace.
Tender moments
Private moments
Where my soul became free---
Where I knew Him fully---

From afar, I had been afraid.
I could not understand.
From afar, I had been ashamed.
From afar, I had been unaware of who He really was.
From afar, I had thought he would hate me
For being me...for being human.

But, when I was drawn into Him,
I desired no longer to be afar; contrarily,
I wanted to be close.
I wanted to know Him.
I wanted to taste Him.
I wanted all of me to have all of Him.

Ronette D. Jacobs

He has made me.
He has shaped me.
He has chastened me.
From up close, I am now His bride
Who waits anxiously for Him.

I am now the apple of His eyes,
And I only want to know Him from up close.
From afar is too removed from the Lover of my soul.
For I am His and He is mine.

Survival

Strangled, mangled, bruised, and left for dead
Seduced, threatened, rejected, and left for dead
Tossed, lost, bossed, and left for dead
Survival

Hungry, thirsty, unsure, yet left for dead
Blind, deaf, dumb, yet left for dead
Burned, battered, broken, yet left for dead
Survival

Stolen, abandoned, hidden; nevertheless, left for dead
Confused, unsure, aimless; nevertheless, left for dead
Misunderstood, accused, refused; nevertheless, left for dead
Survival

Afraid, aloof, and agitated; consequently, left for dead
Tricked, trampled, and troubled; consequently, left for dead
Mangled, molested, miserable; consequently, left for dead
Survival

Tried, tested, testimony: therefore, triumphant
Prayer, praise, power: therefore, peace
Forgiveness, forging, faithful: therefore, favor
Survival

How Would One Know?

How would one know love without experiencing hate?
How would one know joy without having been depressed?
How would one know the end without a beginning?
How would one know acceptance without being rejected?
How would one know power without being frail?

How would one know a friend without having known one's foe?
How would one know the best without having had the worst?
How would one know yesterday had not today been lived?
How would one know comfort without experiencing pain?
How would one know sanity without experiencing insanity?

How would one know warmth without shivering in coldness?
How would one know fruitfulness without having been barren?
How would one know trust without having been betrayed?
How would one know clarity without having been bewildered?
How would one know intimacy without being pretentious?

How would one know knowledge without being misinformed?
How would one know laughter without experiencing sadness?
How would one know beauty without experiencing ugliness?
How would one know belief without knowing unbelief?
How would one know light without having been in the dark?

How would one know fullness without having been hungry?
How would one know silence without encountering noise?
How would one know chastisement without satisfying freedom?
How would one know desperation without perpetual rest?
How would one know revelation without being uncertain?

How would one know courage without having been timid?
How would one know wisdom without having been ignorant?
How would one know aloofness without being close?
How would one know despair without having known jubilation?
How would one know freedom without having been bound?

How would one know?

Who They Say I Am

I don't want to be who they say I am.
I reach deep in my pockets of life, and I pull out lent.
I reach deep in the crevices of my soul,
and I pull out candy wrappers.

I don't want to be who they say I am.
A heart of stone can never grow a flower.
A heart absent of love can never enrich a soul.

I, I don't want to be who they say I am.
Around the corner, I look and I see my future.
Around the curve, I see who they say I am to be.
But, I don't want to be who they say I am.

Thus, it is so that I cannot hide me anymore.
It is so that I can no longer exist behind the dark curtains of life.
It is so that I must come out and never go in again.
It is so that my old life is over.

I don't want to be who they say I am.
But, I must shall't I die.
But, I must be who they say I am to be.

For I know, it came to them way after it came to me,
A vision in my soul, a drawing in my heart.
Therefore, I must be who they say I am,
Because they see me through the eyes of God.

I Slipped

Oh, did I make some gruesome choices…
Oh, but I was pleased…oh, for that moment I was pleased.
My flesh shouted with exuberance as my spirit slowly
plummeted to hell…to darkness.
Oh, how I grieved the One who loved me when no one else did.
Oh, how I sickened the One who had taken me out of hell…
out of death's door.
Dipping, sliding, gliding, and running around…
Telling lies…living a lie…forging the role of holy but being a
full-time hypocrite…
Hating myself…wanting what I had never gotten but from the
wrong place…
Oh, for the delicate moment in time…I was emerged in ecstasy.
But…a flicker of life…a flicker of purpose…a flicker of
destiny…a flicker of truth…a flicker of hell…pierced through
my self-initiated hell.
No longer could I continue…the sweet taste had become
bitter…oh, how bitter it had become.
Life…the one I had now chosen…spat at me…laughed at me
and reminded me of the circle…and the shame and the guilt that
had always poisoned my life.
The fact remained that I had once again made my choices…
my priority.
I pretended to repent…but I went back and back and back…til
no longer could insanity be a part of my life…and soon
I dropped…and I knew death was inevitable.
Who was I to play with God?
Who was I to think that I could be unfaithful to the One who
washed the dirt off me?
Who was I to consider His word not to be true?
I was nothing…
But, again His hand, His mercy, His love…caught me before
death drowned me.
His love washed me. His word told me again…what I had
known before, but this time I could and would no longer fight…

Ronette D. Jacobs

I gave up and I gave in…
My life was never really my own.
Pain had controlled and ruled for long enough.
By grace, I could again walk in the predestined plan.
Surrendering was the epitome of power.
For the predestined plan had long been there
Wrapped in forgiveness, peace, joy, and love.

If You Could See What I See

Off into the deep blue sky,
I see into the horizon---my destiny.
I grab hold of this moment,
For I know not when it shall come again.
No time to waste, no more remembrance
of the things I messed over.

Oh, what a lovely God I serve!
---Who allows me to see His waves crash upon the sand
Oh, what a glorious God I serve!
---Who lets me see the sun's eye pierce through the clouds
Oh, what a marvelous God I serve!
---Who sends His breath of fresh air to awaken and revive

Oh, only if you could see what I see!
In their glorious forms of peaks and heavenly carvings---
Mountains are praising the sovereign God!
Sea grass praises Him as it dances with the wind

Oh, only if you could see what I see!
Pristine beauty etched upon the sky
As the blues and whites intertwine
Clashing and swooshing waves
Pound upon the salty white seashore

Oh, only if you could see what I see!
Sand running through toes of clay
As droplets of saltwater glisten upon me
Gentle breezes intentionally escorting me
to my predetermined destiny

Ronette D. Jacobs

Mother

What a sacrificial lamb!
Giving and never looking back
Working and never growing tired
Praying always for someone else

Oh, dear Mother what a sacrificial lamb!
Loving and always worrying about others' cares
Rejoicing at miraculous moves of God
Gently saying soothing words to bring comfort

Oh, dear Mother what a sacrificial lamb!
Never saying a complaining word
Wanting to see others happy
Overflowing with rivers of love

Oh, dear Mother what a sacrificial lamb!
Humble and never wanting to force her way
Peaceful and gesturing away strife
Serving to help others find their way

Oh, dearest Mother what a sacrificial lamb!
Seeking to serve the Master, truly
Absorbing the richness of His word
Yielding to His holy will

Oh, dearest Mother what a sacrificial lamb!
The Lamb that died for you---
Oh, how you have engulfed His ways

Oh, dearest Mother what a sacrificial lamb!
I could not be if it were not for you---
Oh, sacrificial lamb, for you are called "blessed"!

Taking Nothing for Your Journey

From before time to now, who would have known?
A journey such as this lay before you
No one but God could have known before the beginning of time
That His anointing would pour upon you to spread the gospel

From infancy to now, who would have considered?
A man such as thee from the beginnings to now, heavenly places
No one but God could have known the destiny
of such a shepherd as you
A shepherd who willingly goes beyond the veil for his flock

From years of self-discovery,
who really knew that you would be?
All that God meant for you to be….
from the shadows of the Ancient Paths
To a glorious interlude with the Father and leaving
behind the things of this world
Taking nothing for your journey, you began your destiny

From years of sitting beneath the trees of wisdom and strength
Your journey has been empowered with days of missions
and nights of visions
Tossing aside the traps of this world, you grabbed hold
to riches of the kingdom to come
Immersed in the Word…immersed in His spirit...
immersed in the delicacies of His presence…
He replenishes you for taking nothing for your journey

From the first sermon to today's sermon
and the ones yet manifested
Fire from heaven perpetually fills your soul and heart
Going out into the deep, God has given you all for the journey

Ronette D. Jacobs

For taking nothing for your journey…you have been given
…*EVERYTHING*

His Son, His power, His love, His glory,
His strength, His anointing,
His Spirit, His revelation, His wisdom,
His understanding, His miracles…and *HIM*

For taking nothing for your journey…
Innumerable souls have been yanked away from hell's door
And escorted to eternal life

For taking nothing for your journey…
…a true journey has really begun

What Made You Do It?

From the shore to the farthest distance,
I can see nothing but waves upon waves
What made You create the sand filled
With delicate crystals that glisten on the beach?

Hinging upon exuberating joy as the sun prances,
Being gently pushed along by the caress of the ocean,
I can see tomorrow out there in the midst of the waves.
What made You create a sun that heals the soul?

Smiling within as sprays of water tap upon my face and
Wanting to be lifted high up where the kites rule,
I can see tomorrow, a brighter day…a day with rainbows.
What made you create the spiraling, refreshing winds?

Living waters running from one end to the next
Breathless, engulfed with gratitude of seeing such beauty
Pushing down the sand with every step of the way
What made You create such majestic healing waters?

Oceans powerful, true, and constant!
Empowering waves that wash away clinging sand!
Meditative sounds of healing!
Oh, what made You do it?

Ronette D. Jacobs

Where Do I Go From Here?

No one really knows the way except God
Friend after friend and
Foe after foe
Have all offered a glimmer of guiding light for the way.

Some ways I have walked into.
Some ways I have run from.
Then, there were some that I fell into.

Seconds lost
Minutes lost
Days lost
Weeks lost
Months lost
Years lost

But, here I am wanting to know the way
Wanting never again to waste a day or a moment
Wanting to be strong but my strength fails me
Wanting to live righteously but failing to meet the mark

So, what does my future hold?
Can I recapture what was lost?
Many say no. Many say yes.

I want to know the way.
I need to know the way.

Open up the heavens.
Open up the heavens.

My dear God I am waiting for You!
You said to wait.

26

So, I am waiting and wanting and waiting and wanting.

Trust You?
Oh, yes I know that is the only way.

So, when will You come?
Oh, when will the light guide me down the divine path?
Now, when I can be at peace and full of joy?

Oh, God where do I go from here?

X Chromosome

Y Chromosome

A joining of life
A creation of divineness
Human
Fragile
True
Real
Unique
Precious

Life
Lots of firsts…
A beginning
Discovery…wonder
Learned inadequacies
Taught notions
Choices
Obstacles

Life
Joys
Revelations
Miracles
Pitfalls
Stumbles
Answered Prayers
Unanswered Prayers
Shock of a lifetime
Beauty of changing seasons

Life
Trust
Seeing the unseen
Wise vessels
Acknowledgement of truth
Leaving a legacy
Building a fortress
Protecting sanity
Maintaining dignity
Resting in the foreordained path

Ronette D. Jacobs

A Milestone

Waking up after resting eight years in a comma
Learning to walk again following a long-term paralysis
Graduating from college after suffering a brain injury
Getting pregnant after years of facing infertility

Determination
Motivation
Effort
Perseverance

Speaking fluently and driving following a major stroke
Holding your baby in hand using your prosthetic arm
Stepping out of the car with no injuries after a head-on collision
Making footsteps on foreign soil once overcoming fear of flying

God's great handiwork
A great accomplishment
Blood, sweat, tears, love, and prayers
No matter what, you remained hopeful

Starting a business with a mere five hundred dollars
Moving across country to begin a new fascinating career
Making the winning touchdown during a close-knit game
Marrying one's first love after been apart for forty years

Crossing the finish line
Giving the best effort
Never settling for second best
Expecting a life changing miracle

A child playing a sport when doctors said he would never walk
Reading for the first time at sixty years of age
Fulfilling a life-long dream after praying for thirty years
Being the best in one's career despite all closed doors

30

An extravagant escort of grace and mercy
Soaring choice of optimism and courage
Wonderful working power of Jesus
Incredible tenacity and faith

Be grateful!
Be proud!
Stand tall!
Know the power!

Ronette D. Jacobs

You Didn't Mean To

Harmonious pellets of joy trickled through my sinews.
Melodious raindrops danced across my memory.
Rivers of joy and laughter enriched my soul.

Tremendous puddles of rain enveloped my shoes.
Picturesque flashes of moments packed in memory.
Shivers of loneliness began to quake in my soul.

Calls, cards, and candies packed the threshold.
Pain, poison, and pollution crept through my memory.
Wonders of what could and what should have been lingered.

Angels watching over me...saving me...shielding me...
"I know, hush. You didn't mean to."
It was never a moment that you meant what you said.

Go on. Move on. Strive on.
Tenderness washed away in the cesspool of piercing cries.
Gentleness rubbed away in the abrasiveness of rejection.

"Hush, hush. I know...you didn't mean to."
Remove yourself from that old way.
It is no longer there---no longer available for you to cling to.
"I know. I know. You didn't mean to."

Go forth my love, for my heart sends you life.
Go forth my love, for no strings hold us together.
Go forth my love, for you didn't mean to.

A Flower

A mother is like a flower in many ways.
Her fragrance and color brightens a room.
She cannot be compared to another one.
She maintains her strength through all seasons.
Whether her children are sick, rejoicing, or depressed,
She is there.

She is appreciated for being the family's flower.
Like a flower, she doesn't say much,
But she captivates onlookers.
Her presence brings great joy to the lives of her children.
She refuses to retreat to a corner
When the obstacles of life come.

Her unconditional love reflects the Creator.
Just from watching her, many can learn life's greatest lessons.
Her beauty and steadfastness are to be admired.
Gazing upon her life, wisdom is attained.
She places the desires of others before her own.
She wears her love like a beautiful spring dress.

She is a flower.

Ronette D. Jacobs

A Journey

It's morning...the blades of grass are full of tears
A fresh beginning
Where yesterday has faded
A new beginning...where the end has been a great thing

Refused, rejected, returned, and replaced
Unnoticed, unacceptable, unprepared, and unappreciated
Misunderstood, misconstrued, misrepresented, and mishandled
Petrified, purified, but placid
Reckless, rotten, yet redeemed

It's noon...the heat is rising and the blades crave tears
A road divided...which path to take
Where tomorrow is unknown
A pause...where the end is not noticed

Bitter, bruised, but better
Callous, crying, but calm
Excluded, examined, but exonerated
Tested, tried, tempted, but tamed

It's night...the moon has spoken and the blades seek solace
An unveiling...a surrendering
A closed door...an open window
A pilgrimage...a new life

Meditative and miraculous
Learning and loving
Kindness and kept
Powerful and purposeful

A journey

Breath of My Heart

How dare you enter into a place
That has been filled with so much pain!
How dare you come along and show me what laughter is!
How dare you penetrate these concrete walls
Which have kept me safe!

Who sent you with such a loving heart?
Who sent you with such a generous spirit?
Who sent you with such a gentle love?

Why do you love me in such a way?
Why do you care if my day was great?
Why do you desire to be a part of my life?

Off guard, you caught me.
Consumed with busyness, you interrupted me.
Shut off from intimacy, you rescued me.

Breath of my heart
Tender and dear
Breath of my heart
Humble and true

Breath of my heart
Powerful
Breath of my heart
Unleashed

Breath of my heart
Amazing
Real
Everlasting
Unconditional

Ronette D. Jacobs

808

Refuse to be like Lot's wife.
Embrace this new season.
Regrets are stripped of their control.

Sorrow over what has been lost no longer matters.
Retake of images has been deleted.
Power of painful places has been stripped.

A new day has come!
A glorious world awaits the new footsteps.
All baggage has been deposited.

What was can never be again!
Fresh heavenly dew is falling.
Expectations are springing forth!

A worthwhile new beginning…worthwhile
Pages of blank sheets waiting to be filled…blank
Rivers of rapid new waters are running…new

Wisdom is crisp and ready for embarking.
Experiences are at this time ready to be tools.
Memories have been washed and set for reshaping.

It is now the time.
It is now no longer before.
It is now a time to move forward.

The former season has ended.
It is harvest time.
A new beginning!

The Last Day

What would I do because
I have not seen you today?
How could I leave without having seen
Your wonderful smile today?

It would be impossible to leave because
I did not hear you call my name today.
I would try to stay longer just
to smell your fragrance of love.

It couldn't be my last day because
I didn't get a hug from you today.
I would fight to stay to have
your kisses upon my cheeks.

My screams of halt would pierce the sky because
I would want one more chance to have you hold my hands.
I would pray for another lifetime just to spend
It with you---loving you.

Today could not be my last day
because I am not with you.
My breath cannot fade away
because you are not near my side.

And with you is where I want to be on my last day.
And with you is where I want to be now and forever.

Ronette D. Jacobs

Forgiveness

An unimaginable powerful force of life
An ocean that brings freedom
A key that breaks the chains of bondage

A way to eliminate all effects of strife
Freedom from the need to retaliate
Bondage of destructive memories are forsaken

A door to a new beginning
An unleashing of fresh thoughts
A true fruit of authentic love

Forsaking the need to live in those painful feelings
Honoring one own's health and soul
Accepting grace to operate beyond one's own strength

Realizing humanity is flawed
Recognizing loving others will require death of self
Being vulnerable enough to release others

Trusting not in emotions
Living above what is seen
Knowing the cost is intimacy with God

Giving freely as it has been given
Escorting the moment to the throne
Living in peaceful reverence

Trusting that all will be worked out in the end
Appreciating one's battles are never fought alone
Understanding that forgiving is a matter of choice

Innocence

Born into this world, unaware of evil
Full of hopes, dreams, desires, and beliefs
Possessing a smile that can light up the darkest room
Full of glee and His glory

Knowing no touch of pain or the residue that it leaves
Ignorant to shame and guilt
Full of life and love
Expecting the best

Has never been spoiled by the unwarranted touch of a predator
Seeking the good in all people
Still believing and trusting
Full of questions, anticipations, and discoveries

Endowed with pure penetrating eyes that
sparkle like diamonds
Laughter streaming from a heart that holds
no betrayals or disappointments
Treasurable tears of joy which dance down the cheekbone
To a lap where nothing or no one has entered

Dumbfounded to humiliation and degradation
Still understanding that life has no limitations
Running through the meadows of life
Letting His breeze blow upon the days
Yet to realize fully that tomorrow will be
An even more precious jewel because He lives

Innocence

Ronette D. Jacobs

Just *one* Little Mistake

Oh, we think of the moment as so---right
Just *one* little mistake, a slip of the tongue, a slip of the foot,
a slip of the hand
A memory that leaps forward into the present
Just *one* little mistake
So often we make you, but we can't move beyond you
Answers from the left, from the right, from within,
and from without
But, to no avail, you are still there
Haunting us, calling us, trailing us,
reminding us of our human frailty
Moments that can never be fixed or erased
Time comes to heal
Time comes to remove
Time comes to cover
But, will there ever be a day when the mistake
is no longer fresh?
When will everyone forget what we have done,
where we have lived, what we have said,
and most importantly how we have lived?
Just *one*---just *one*---little mistake that pulls a person
off the ordained track to a track of unfruitfulness.
A mistake
Can it ever be turned to a miracle?
We can only hope
That life will have a change of heart, and
That moment will somehow become something great.
Until then---we sit and hope and believe there---
Around the corner---there is a brighter day
waiting to heal us of our past
To correct our wrongs
To cover our failures
To escort us on to our journey of miracles!

Her Journey

Just yesterday, she was riding a tricycle
with plastic yellow, red, and blue tassels dangling
from the metal handlebars.
The world of bobby socks and frilly dresses
The world of bonnets and great smiles
Then you came along and stole her white beautiful dress.
It was never to be the same, stained forever.

Washed away with the tides are
the dreams of a little girl
Washed away with the sand are
the days of tenderness and protection
From then to now

Who would have thought
That such a time would come
When her insides felt like they had been glazed
with a scouring pad?
Who would have thought that the little girl
Who loved life would soon hate life and all the people in it?

Someone saw her. Someone had to see her.
But, no one whispered... "This is the way..."
From night to day, from day to night...
a wilderness became her life.

Nothing to cling to and nothing to hope for
Just a journey that others spoke of but none of her own
How would she get it? When would she get it?
From where would she get it?
Some said never. Some said soon. Some said May.
Some said when the change of life began.
Yet, her journey never came.

Ronette D. Jacobs

From one pillow to the next,
From one broken dream to the next,
From one empty house to the next,
From one leaking faucet to the next,
Her journey ended…on a gurney.

Life seeped away.
The blood gone.
Nothing more.
Life drained.
Life stolen.
Potential.

A Wedding Promise

My promise to you is eternal
because our spirits shall meet again in heaven.
I cannot promise you the world
because it doesn't belong to me,
but upon your honorable request,
my heart, my mind, and my body you may have.

I cannot promise you fancy jewels,
but I can promise to be your very own jewel.
I cannot give you the biggest diamond,
but I can give you the biggest part of me, my heart.
I cannot buy you the finest mansion,
but I can make you a home full of love
and peace to come to daily.

I cannot promise you the latest business news,
but I can promise you two ears to listen and
two arms to embrace you to share in your day.
I cannot promise you that I will never be upset with you,
but I can promise you unconditional love.

I cannot promise you the most expensive fur coat to cover you,
but I can promise to bathe you daily in prayers and blessings.
I cannot promise you that I will never make a mistake,
but I can promise you that I will never leave you nor my God.

Nobody Told Me

Somewhere along the way, they forgot
To tell me who you would be
That you would come in disguise to kill me
That you would come in disguise to erase me from the earth

But nobody told me
How could they not see me?
Or did they see me as I grew from
a seed to a stem to a budding flower?
Did they miss my presence?
Or did they think you would not bother me?

But nobody told me
That you would come to steal my innocence;
That you would come to steal my hopes;
That you would come to steal my joy; and
That you would come to steal my soul.

But nobody told me
That all the shiny things from you become dull;
That all the gold becomes a tainted brown;
That all your diamonds are just sheer glass; and
That all the "I love you's" were twisted tales.

But nobody told me
That your plan was to halt the plans of my Creator;
That your plans were to steal my praise;
That your plan was to cause my death to come before time; and
That you hated me…every single part of me.

But nobody told me
That God created me in His image;
That God would love me no matter how filthy my life had been;

That Jesus' blood was enough;
That I would never be alone;
That God wanted to protect me; and
That God loved me.

But nobody told me.

Pain

Who was it that thought up this wretched place?
How is it that this hole can reach so deep?
From a crevice in my soul, it stems
to the farthest reaches of the universe.
Trying to survive…trying to hide it…has consumed my life.
One day I woke up, and I was no longer me,
but the pain that resided in me.
I got loss in the tumultuous never ending swirls of recovery---
pain---recovery---pain.
When, oh, when will it end?
A life like no other---
For it was not I that opened this door,
Yet, I continued through it seeking those things
Which continued my pain.
So this day, I seek to be detached from my pain, my shame,
my guilt, and my past.
This life…this life…this *more abundant life* is what I seek.
Not yesterday's disgusting rumblings,
Nor the voices of darkness,
But, I desire the Rock and the Source and the Shield.
Who will remove this pain from me,
So like an eagle I can be free to soar?
To see the beauty of a rainbow
To feel the true breath of God
To live in the promised freedom
To dance upon the waves of the ocean
To enjoy the unexpected love of a dear loved one
To glance upon His reflection in me and *be*---
Pain, be gone I say!
No longer do I need you clinging to my soul and
reminding me of who I used to be and
what you think I cannot be.
To hell, I send you!

Over you, I release the blood of Jesus!
Over you, I release the love of God!
Pain, I commit you to death!
I live! I love! I live! I love!

Precious Moments

Never taken for granted
Can never be relived
Can never be duplicated
Precious moments

Finite in detail
Personalized from heaven
Generated to show His sovereignty
Precious moments

So tender and so true
Fragile in nature
So perfect and so intimate
Precious moments

Breathe them in
Soak in them
Surround oneself in them
Precious moments

Realize they are not in the fabricated moments
Know they are not present in self-arranged destinies
Understand these moments cannot be contained
Precious moments

Silver and gold cannot purchase them
Titles and positions cannot earn them
Old money nor new money can buy them
Precious moments

Given to all regardless of class, race, or privilege
Dressed in uniqueness for each special one
Formulated to leave a deep impression on the heart
Precious moments

Still there in the memory at life's end
Still able to bring joy upon reflection
Still powerful enough to connect souls
Precious moments

Ronette D. Jacobs

Truth

What is it? That thing they call the truth.
Nobody told us about the truth.
Is it something good or something bad?
Can I buy it in the store? If I can,
I know I can get it at a dollar store.

Where does it come from?
How do people get it?
Do I have to be empty to eat it?
What will it do for me?
Will it send me somewhere?

The truth comes through the crevices of life
where the cement has tried to hide it.
The truth comes through the sunset
that forces the darkness away.
It has its own power. It is anointed.
It heals. It destroys all falsehoods.
It empowers. It thrusts one forward.
It takes the shackles off the ankles of the slaves.

The truth comes like lightning,
but it also comes in like a gentle lamb.
No more destruction in its presence.
No more shame in its presence.
No more fear in its presence.
Nothing can hold it back.

The truth---will you drink of it? Will you eat of it?
The truth
cannot be hidden.
It must come.

Waiting to Behold You

Each day away from you,
I think of how I treasure you.
You really are *heaven-sent*,
and I know there is no other like you.

What we have surpasses the ordinary "I love you".
I have waited patiently on my Father, my God, and my Savior.
He has told me that I may give myself unto YOU fully.
So without wavering or doubting, I am yours.

I am yours to adore, to love, and to cherish.
You are mine to respect and to honor.
Everything that I have is yours.
Nothing can penetrate this love.

We serve a perfect God
who is faithful enough
to walk, guide, lead, and cover us.
This day, this hour, this moment,
and forever, I want to behold you.

With all that God has given unto me,
you are my most perfect gift from above.
Through you, I can love God even more.
Waiting to behold you.

Ronette D. Jacobs

Missing You

Between you and me, there were
----no secrets.
With each other, we flowed with what
made our hearts ache and
what made our hearts sing.
I miss you so!

You kept me true to myself.
You held me accountable for yesterday.
My deepest, darkest days were lightened
in your warm hugs.
My gruesome moments of fears and abuse
were whispered in your ears.
I miss you so!

If anyone should have ever asked after I was gone,
you would have been the only one to tell my story.
You held my dreams between your
whiteness of hope and aspiration.
You could hold the honor of best friend.
Truly, you are missed.

Had life been simpler and
Perhaps if providence had been our third chord,
Who is to say what could have been
Had not the *sabotager* of peace and love drawn a sword.
Oh, how I miss you so!

Ravaged

"Sit down!"
"Get over here."
"That's not what I told you to do!"
"Where is my food?"
"Where do you think you are going?"
"I'll kill you first."

"Are you retarded or something?"
"You are so stupid!"
"Dummy. Hey, dummy."
"You mean nothing to me."

Oh, Lamb of God,
Let Your love come to my rescue.
Wash me in Your healing balm.
Let my soul be refreshed in You.

Oh, Lamb of God,
Let me not be swallowed whole.
Let not my rescue be held up any longer.
Open paradise to me.
Show me the straight and narrow path once more.

Oh, Lamb of God,
Oh, Creator of my very being,
Free me from this captive place.
Surrender me to a place unknown.

Oh, Lamb of God,
Oh, merciful Jehovah!
Loose my soul from this barren prison.
Deliver me to the rivers of living water.

Ronette D. Jacobs

Come now,
Oh, Lord!
Come, now!

Let me be free again!
Let my soul ascend!
Let my heart know real love!

Pleasantries

Dwelling in the house of the Lord!
Sweet wonders of Your mysteries
Glorious displays of Your love
Wondrous ways of Your kindness

Dwelling in the house of the Lord!
Melodious melodies capturing my heart
Sounds of heaven raining
Only oneness exists in You!

Dwelling in the house of the Lord!
Clarion calls piercing the atmosphere
Full freedom emerging from side to side
Relentless pursuit of You

Dwelling in the house of the Lord!
For You make my heart glad!
Resounding praises drenching the air
Glorifying the goodness of You!

Oh, how pleasant it is!

Ronette D. Jacobs

Reveling in His Truth

You are loved!
You are forgiven!
His promises are true!

He will never leave you!
You are the apple of His eyes!
You are more than a conqueror!

You have been delivered from all fears!
You have been forgiven of all your iniquities!
His spirit will reveal those things hidden!

Man cannot destroy what God created!
All power is really in your hands!
Your words can bring down kings!

You live before an audience of One!
Everything you need can be found in Him!
His words are true and forever!

He will never condemn you!
He welcomes your praise!
His delight is found in you!

God is righteousness!
Only He can restore a soul!
There is forever joy in His presence!

For Once, I Loved

Dipping
Tripping
Gripping
Bellowing
Flipping
---Astonished at the pain a human heart can endure.
---You walked in like silk and crept away like a snake.
---You amazed parts that had never ever before lived.
---Secretly, you played Russian roulette with my heart.
For once, I loved
Hoping
Trusting
Pouring
Glorying
Soaring
Landing flat in a pool of perilous pain

Ronette D. Jacobs

Worship Explosion

Fierce fire from the brazen altar
Surrendered souls and hearts
Shouts of wonder!
Shouts of praise!
Wanting to be caught up in You!

Looking nowhere else
Knowing that You are the one true Love!
Anticipating being with You!
Giving all the love of the heart

Leaps and dances of joy
Drowning in the goodness of You
Enveloped in the presence of the Almighty!
Grateful for the breath of life

Caring only what You think
All else seems meaningless
Only You deserve the praise!
You are mightier than any mountain!

Amazed by Your wonder!
Awestruck by Your goodness!
Excited about Your love!
The beauty of You!

THE Creator of the heaven AND the earth!
Breathtaking Lover!
Grand beyond human imagination!
Drowning in the depths of Your love

Never!
Never!
Never!
---*shall the rocks cry out for me!*

Becoming

Life serves a hard-boiled egg…
It can be eaten alone…
It can be eaten in a salad…
Hidden beneath a veil
Faceless
Invisible
Wanting desperately to come forth
Anxiously waiting beneath hope
Believing there is something more
Desiring to see beyond the fog
Anticipating a transformative moment
Knowing that a greatness rests within
That the day has gone
Yearning to endure the past no more
Hoping for a sunrise etched permanently in the sky
Unnoticed
Misunderstood
Crystal thoughts wanting to be shared
Searching for a heart that can comprehend
Envisioning a love that cares
Enough to listen…enough to ask
Soon it shall come forth
Becoming…

Ronette D. Jacobs

Yesterday

You came forth with a blank slate.
Willingly, I filled you with thoughts
That leaped from the other side of me.

You seemed so real…so forever.
The pain I felt did not want to die.
Oh, how I hoped yesterday would be gone.

You made me feel like there was no way out.
I could not see beyond the sky of that day nor
The nervous hope that a tomorrow would come.

But, you came back again today
Wanting and looking for that question.
No more we say! No more!

Yesterday died with the old wine.
Yesterday's heart could no more forever live.
Yesterday's sadness has been removed.

Yesterday has no power over tomorrow.
Yesterday has been washed away.
Yesterday is a forgotten place.

Grateful

A gift from the human heart
A supernatural force
An empowering attribute
A life filled with reciprocity

Grateful
Sacrifices
Prayers
Love
Kindness

Grateful
Thoughts
Feelings
Concerns
Desires

Grateful
Hopes
Purpose
Memories
Compassion

Grateful
Wisdom
Experiences
Pathways
Choices

Grateful
Time
Talents
Gifts
Wonders

Give Away

Pure
Precious
Innocent
Violet

Tender
Kept
Gentle
Loving

Priceless
Joy
Holy
Powerful

Strength
Adoration
Sanity
Wonder

Destiny
Soul
Treasures
Delight

Promises
Birthright
Position
Protection

Etched Place

Before the foundation of the earth,
God created you just for me.
He knitted you in His womb and fashioned you
To cover me, protect me, and shield me.

He knew I would need your kisses,
Your hugs, your affection, and
Most of all your genuine unconditional love.
He knew there would be nights
When nothing could satisfy my heart's cries but you.

He knew there would be days
When the storms ceased to stop
For He created you, just for me.
Who would think that the absence of you
Would leave such a depth of void within?

Too many days, months, and years went by without you…
Too many nightmares, unwanted, and unwarranted touches…
Too many glares, stares, and dares…
Too many drifts, cliffs, and regrets…

For those years without you
Were too long to wait to know you.
A thread of emptiness was woven
Through each circumstance.

God had created a place
Just for you in my heart.
For you see, no one could replace
Your permanently etched place.
No one.

Ronette D. Jacobs

Searching

Beyond myself, there is a place,
A place formed before my birth.
In this place, I can be more.
In this place, I can soar.

I desperately seek this place.
Its need is resembled on my face.
In running this challenging race,
I need to find this solace.

My soul thirsts for this place.
No other drink can quench this thirst.
No other morsel can fill this hunger.
I crave to find this succor.

I traveled north and south;
I could not find it there.
I traveled east and west;
I could not find it there.

Oh, where is this place?
Oh, mighty nature does not hold it!
Oh, stellar positions do not hold it!
Oh, the fairest of lovers do not hold it!

Within is where it is.
Deep within the sinews-
Deep within the silent whispers-
Intently away from the noise-

There is such a place,
Perfect and true.
There is such a place
That can make me new.

Life

Birth
Tears of joy
Wonderful tumbles
Twilight eyes

Fingers the size of candy corn
Skin so silky---such an honor to behold
Heartfelt belly roll laughter
Unexplainable depths of love

Waves of discovery
Moments of evolution
Thrills of riding a new bike
Rollercoaster luminous growth

String bean legs sprouting
Eclipsed by the unknown and innocence
Raptured in the wonders of newness
Bewildered by life changes

Valleys and peaks of adolescence
Growing into a stranger in the midst
Challenging life boundaries
Finding the predestined path

Charging through rigorous academic arenas
Absorbing and considering profound mindsets
Coming to terms with personal philosophies
Crossing milestones to begin another

Divine intersection of one true love
Committed to a shared life and destiny
Hoping to accomplish all life's goals
Anticipating a well-lived path

Ronette D. Jacobs

Rejoicing in a new generation
Humbled by the miracle of birth
Jointly excited about the new one
Facing the true meaning of life

The becoming of switched roles
Loving memories tiptoeing away
A body awakening to time's influence
Embracing that there is a greater life beyond

Another Chance

God's grace permits to some---

    another chance at life's journey

Seeing the power of healing transform one's body---

    made by the fearless and wonderful God

Revelation is done---

    listening to God's guiding and gentle love

Dots amazingly joined together---

    to bring about a very expected end

With such a perfect Lover---

    who knows every hair count

Bringing all of the infinite minutes together---

    to show how He can make *all* things work

    together for the good

His amazing ways can bring such beautiful angels ---

    from decades past to show His love

Only El Elyon can intertwine---

    His knowledge of man to reveal true purpose

Only Jehovah-Rophe can restore---

    His divine child's mind, body, soul, and spirit

Only Jehovah-Raah can guide---

    His creation to a new beginning, a new place, a new time

Cut Short

Wrong place
Summer party
Football game
Appomattox River
Texting – "c u soon"
Senseless games
Hazing out of control
An argument gone too far
Wrong person
Sitting on the porch
Playing god with drugs
A day in the park
Stray bullets
Alcohol and the driving wheel
An unbuckled seatbelt
Route 58
Wrong motive
Succumbing to the suicide lie – "no way out"
Boston marathon
A walk home from the store
Getting off the school bus
Shooting some hoops
A drive to the shopping mall
Meaningless territorial strife
Wrong time
A stolen
       Destiny
A stolen
       Hope
A stolen
       Future
A stolen
       Purpose
Cut short...a HUMAN life!

Unforgiveness

A possible place in human strength
Not realizing the magnitude of grace given
Deep wounds, deep pain, deep betrayal

Seeing you, opens deep crevices
Days have passed; months have crept away
Years have fleeted as stolen moments
Holding on to what should have been let go

Sipping cups of bitterness
Taking deep bites of resentment
Wearing a robe of hostility
Partnering with anger

Struggling to move beyond the scars
Needing to be released from the darkness
Hoping to have the heart restored

Not wanting to see you
Not wanting to hear your voice
Not wanting to be in your presence

Wanting to let go
Wanting to move on
Wanting a new memory

Bound in chains
Frozen in time
Physiological disruption
Drinking poison

Destiny thief
Calling robber
Purpose prison
Freedom killer

Ronette D. Jacobs

A Garden to Behold

Strategic needs, desires, and hopes
Focused selections and placement
Sowing and reaping and sowing and reaping

Resplendent heavenly wonders
Uniquely formed and colored
Fragrances giving the world much joy

Kneeling on a soft pillow
Protecting nose, eyes, and mouth
Trusting the seeds to grow

> Hyacinths
> Butterfly Bushes

Amazed by their elegance
Attracting delicate and unique butterflies
Worrisome weeds winding through

> Gladioli
> Oriental Lilies

Projecting peace
Violet, red, yellow, white
Working with hands

> Hostas
> Japanese Forestgrass

Bold, balanced, and beautiful
Green and self-propelling
Pruning and purging deadness

Roses
Tulips

Beautifully shaped
Yellow, red, white
Fresh fragrances of earth

Hydrangeas
Plentiful and pleasing
Blue, purple, white
An etched memory from childhood

Azaleas

Resilient and resolute
Timely fashioned
Power packed plant food

Purple Heart flowers

Powerful, progressive, and purple
Thrilled to see new growth
Spreading love across the garden

-all together-

Gazing eyes fixated on your beauty
All glory given to the One who gave you increase
Fulfilling life's growth cycle

Giving credence to digging in the earth
Inspiring humility because of your beauty
Worthy of the sweat, grunts, and aches
A garden to behold!

Ronette D. Jacobs

Angels

As I sit on my porch watching the sun set,
Knowing that you are there brings me comfort;
I cannot imagine how all of my life will be yet.

Though, I am confident each step of the way,
You will be a gentle guide.
For you are with me each and every day.

When the frigid uncertain moments arrive,
You kindly take my trembling hand
And watch over me to keep me alive.

Upon the tumultuous seas of my life,
Your presence calms the waves
And protects me from treacherous strife.

Whatever the tapestry of this great life brings,
You work through the knots in the threads
As you bring great honor to the King of all Kings.

Angels watching over me I cannot deny.
Angels watching over me I cannot deny.
In every circumstance, they are my greatest ally!

Can't You See?

The unfolding of the human heart displays
A heart's need for love and acceptance.
That I, like you, am beautiful.
That I, like you, am unique.

How dare you walk by like you do not see me!
How dare you enter my space and
not acknowledge my human presence!
How dare you see my humanity stolen and
you say not a word nor shed a tear!

Can't you see I am real?
Can't you see that I matter too?
Can't you see that we are connected?
For I, like you, am human also!

Take away my existence, and your life will be unlivable.
Take away my life, and you too will soon die.
Take away my presence, and your soul will long for depth.
Take away my breath, and you too, will cease to breathe.

Can't you see that I am a contributor in this universe?
Can't you see we are more alike than foes?
Can't you see that our destinies are intertwined?
Can't you see that I am not a fleeting thought?

IF only you would fear less,
IF only you would expand your heart,
IF only you would want to escape the lies, AND
IF only you would drink the truth,

You would see!

Ronette D. Jacobs

Wake Up

Tick, tock, tick, tock, tick, tock
It's over---no more time
A quick whisper
A long breath
life

Tick, tock, tick, tock, tick, tock
The minute hand---the hour hand
Seconds, minutes, hours
life

Tick, tock, tick, tock, tick, tock
Choices---*the ultimate form of power*
Where will you go? How will you live today?
life

Tick, tock, tick, tock, tick, tock
Truth or dare
Faith or fear
life

Tick, tock, tick, tock, tick, tock
Days, months, years
A quick wind---a quick impact
life

Tick, tock, tick, tock, tick, tock
A legacy—leaving a blessing? a burden?
Mending souls---ripping hearts
life

Tick, tock, tick, tock, tick, tock
Powerful pioneer---prevalent procrastinator
Aware of time---waster of breath
life

Tick, tock, tick, tock, tick, tock
A journey for all
A great ride for some
life

Tick, tock, tick, tock, tick, tock
Reciprocal waves
Moving beyond self
life

Ronette D. Jacobs

Humbled by Your Grace

When I look back through the years,
I am humbled by Your grace.
When I examine the ways I have lived my life,
I am humbled by Your grace.

Upon thinking of all the ways I have hurt You,
I am humbled by Your grace.
As I reflect on the choices I have made,
I am humbled by Your grace.

Considering the blessings You have still bestowed upon me,
I am humbled by Your grace.
Honoring the precious moments I have been given,
I am humbled by Your grace.

Realizing the ways You have protected me,
I am humbled by Your grace
When I should have died several times over,
I am humbled by Your grace.

Intentionally choosing the wrong way,
I am humbled by Your grace.
Swayed away from Your presence,
I am humbled by Your grace.

At times, I caused more pain than joy,
I am humbled by Your grace.
As I lived just for me,
I am humbled by Your grace.

When I see my life today,
I humbled by Your grace.
You have turned my darkness into light.
I am humbled by Your grace.

You have turned my mess into miracles.
I am humbled by Your grace.
You have worked those evil things together for a greater good.
I am humbled by Your grace.

It has been Your grace that has carried me.
It has been Your grace that has kept me.
It has been Your grace that has saved me.
And it has been Your grace that has made me whole.

Ronette D. Jacobs

Nesting Places

Surrounded by manicured exquisite lawns
Well-skilled architecture developed abodes
Grounds implanted with automatic sprinklers
Garages extended to hold multiple toys

Surrounded by worn and patchy grass
A shingle or shutter missing here or there
Yards filled with discarded rejects
Cars parked out in the elements of nature

Children playing freely and joyfully
Paved sidewalks and neighborly exchanges
Quiet and tranquil evenings upon porches
Joggers, walkers, and strollers take to the street

Children dash between speeding cars and stray bullets
Cracked sidewalks and isolated neighbors
Tense and alert sittings upon porches
Crowded corners and hidden eyes take to the street

City leaders and workers favor and honor
Nesting places are at the top of the list
Monies contributed freely to the well-being
Street signs and safe lighting delight

City leaders and workers overlook with a wink
Nesting places are constantly ignored
Dry and empty with no hope in sight
Old or absent signs and dimly lit streets

Filled with great farmers' markets and coffee shops
Fine customer service and human contact
Welcoming opportunities and ready for service
A race to enter such nesting places

Drenched in liquor stores and payday and title loans devourers
A bulletproof glass welcome and a denigrating purchase
Absent human contact and burdensome grunts
Overlooked havens---discounted purpose

Equal nesting places for all humans
Equal nesting places for all peoples
Equal nesting places for all citizens
Equal nesting places for all families
Equal nesting places for all taxpayers
Equal nesting places for each individual

Ronette D. Jacobs

Food Deserts

Granny Smith juice packed apples
Sweet reddish watermelons
Potassium filled ready bananas
Delightful kiwi and papayas

Green collards and kale galore
Corn on the cob ready for any table
Carrots crafted for a king
Jumbo sweet potatoes

America's beginning...farming
America's beginning...eating directly from the land
America, can you see us?

We are all your children.
Take us back to the earth.
For we need your rich resources.

We can no longer live off
Processed or steroid induced creations.
Our corners need full harvest zones.

Let not our class, culture, race, or ethnicity
Kill off the next generations by limited living.
Release concern and action, America!

Eliminate dry, barren, empty, and wanting places!
Fill these voids with vivid colors and tasty jewels from
Nature that are packed with life giving nutrients.

Let not another generation be poisoned by poverty,
Poisoned by ignorance, neglect, and abandonment.
May we return to our truest selves: nature.

America, empower all people to embrace life!
America, no longer deny your citizens of their futures!
America, distribute your wealth of nature's abundance to all!

Ronette D. Jacobs

Is Anybody Listening?

To the precious little ones whose
faces are covered in last week's grime?
To the husband who wants to stop watching
that filth but can't?
To the teen who can't seem to find
the divine path for him/herself?

To the daughter who really wants
to fly instead of walk?
To the child carrying life's burden bestowed
upon him by an overly stressed adult?
To the overlooked widow who sits day
after day looking out the window?

To the single woman valuing her selective singleness?
To the man eating cat food once more for his supper?
To the overworked and undervalued stay-at-home Mom?

To the one who has all of life luxuries
yet displays absolutely no joy?
To the one sitting on the same church row
that needs help buying gas just to get home?
To the frightened one overtaken by
dark dreams and tentacles of alcohol?

To the one who can't love out of an empty deep well?
To the one fixated on final exams and striving for perfection?
To the one who has stopped singing from the heart?

To the child who lashes out in anger
to console the divide of a loving home?
To the one who seeks purpose
after being married for thirty years?
To the man who is ready to grow up
and the world won't let him?

Can you hear their cries?
Will you listen?
Will you stop?
Will you react?
Will you respond?
Will you pass by?
Is anybody listening?

Ronette D. Jacobs

An Extraordinary Man

I was handcrafted from perfection into human form
Delicately created for a mandatory mission
Set apart for His spectacular display
A mind filled with ingenious miracles

I am shaped in handsomeness and beauty
Empowered in super strength and resilience
Full of wisdom and creative depth
Marked for success and service

Fully, I am drenched in love from head to toe
Enhanced by submission to Him
Guided by gentle whispers
Equipped to wreak havoc on darkness

Boldly, I have been anointed to lead and guide
Established to show forth praise
Able to equip many generations
Motivated to produce and leave a legacy

Indeed, I am a true and strong provider
Able to face personal shortcomings
Secure enough to make changes
Giving my all to those dearest to me

Yes, I am unhindered by fear and failure
Not shaken by disaster or limitations
Intimate with the greater One
Unashamed of the true Source

Intentionally, I am wrapped in strong discipline
Showered in loving honor
Capable of showing love
Guided by morals of a higher code

For yes, I am able to face life's dilemmas
Predestined to blaze a path in history
Strong enough to be gentle
Creative in thought and actions

Hence, I am never diminished by my setbacks
Never distracted by setups
Impeccable wonder of this earth
Yes, I am an extraordinary man!

Ronette D. Jacobs

An Extraordinary Woman

I am exceptional and spectacular.
Everything about me has been fearfully and wonderfully created.
Indeed, there exists no one in the universe like me.
Behold, I was crafted for a divine purpose.

Boldness and confidence are my friends.
A hopeful heart and a focused mind are my allies.
Glass ceilings shatter when I enter the room.
My dress of humility escorts me along my path.

Mirrors shimmer in accolades in my flowing presence.
Worthless things cannot hold my attention.
No entanglements of sin or bondage can keep me in prison.
My mouth speaks forth blessings beyond me.

My thoughts are yielded to His thoughts.
I am delighted in serving, loving, and giving.
I lay down my life, hopes, dreams, fears, and plans.
Diligence and passion rest within me.

Never is there a need for comparison.
My life course has been charted.
I have no need to be afraid or resentful.
All I need is supplied in Him.

A victor's cloak is my outerwear.
A soul of creativity has been bestowed upon me.
Days of love and nights of peace are my wonderland.
Strength and power are wrapped in my belly.

I cannot be held down or held back.
Settling is never a place of ponderance.
A door is slammed in the face of regrets.
Destiny is woven into my blood and veins.

Impeccable beauty and shocking gentleness
Glorious gratitude and everlasting joy
Gifted beyond human measure
I am an extraordinary woman!

Ronette D. Jacobs

Wonders of Summer

Raging lawnmowers swinging blades through lush green grass
Delightful, churning musicals played by ice cream trucks
Buzzing bees in search of sweet dining places
Soaring, sizzling, and enticing smells of grand barbecues

Flickering miracle and delight of amazing fireflies
Metamorphosed, bold, beautiful, and vivid butterflies
Racing to devour an ice cream cone before it melts
Shattering thunder and piercing lightning clashing

Captivating spectators enraptured by a bold rainbow
Children running jubilantly through summer's freedom
Blazing nights sitting under the moon and stars
Salty water droplets tantalizing the tongue during a beach swim

Clear blue skies and ripples of simmering heat
Blossoming trees, plants, and flowers covering the earth
Fragrances of honeysuckle and roses pleasing the air
Delicate skin transformed by the glowing summer rays

Daring days and nights of splendor
Elongated days filled with great laughter
Pleasantly warm nights promoting long beach walks
Cold, delicious watermelon and flavored frozen popsicles

Rainbow shades of electrifying fireworks
Delicious lemonade quenching summer thirsts
Appreciating freedom and honoring our fallen heroes
Embracing quick sky showers to cool off the earth

A time of near and distant travels exploring the world
Tapestries of family reunions joining hearts and lives
Packed isles filled with nervous grooms and stellar brides
Times of great love, great wonders, and blazing memories

I Am

I believe
> that I was handcrafted by the Almighty and Holy God!

I believe
> that His spirit breathes through my inner being!

I believe
> the unadulterated truth about myself!

Therefore,
> I am free to be myself!
> I am fearfully and wonderfully made!
> I am cleansed and saved by the blood of the Lamb,
> freed from all guilt and shame!

I am
> more than able to do all that the Lord requires of me
> through His unmerited grace and favor!

I am
> the resonating depth of physicality, spiritual, and
> emotional richness!

I am
> at rest in who I am!

For I am who I am!
For I am His most precious child!
The exception is me, a unique, one in a trillion jewel,
reflecting the greatest wonder of the world!

Myself!

Ronette D. Jacobs

Trailblazers

Sneaking through swamps and traveling by night
Having grown tired of seeing others bound
Giving of self to bring many to a place of freedom
Strong in heart, body, mind, soul, and spirit

Gently praying and setting aside her dreams
Walking beside a man of great courage
Maintaining dignity and honor despite life's trials
Fiercely believing in a better tomorrow

Accepting the call to beautify one's own
Finding a way to make beauty shine even more
Prevailing in inventions to transform
Becoming a millionairess before times allowed

Practice has made all things perfect
Resilient and relentless in pursuit of being herself
Drawing others to her freedom of expression
Setting the records straight across all courts

Born with melodious and powerful ranges
Gracing stages unlike none before
Standing before noble dignitaries
Sharing with powerful angels and ancestors

A humbled beginning disguised as destiny
Communicating in distinct and transparent ways
Giving of love and empathy to empower others
Transforming lives through the world of media

Gifted, caring, graceful, brave, and stylish
Elegant, bold, confident, beautiful and smart
Transforming America's view of beauty
True strength alongside a powerful office*mate*

A global source of diverse knowledge
An intelligent force and passionate heart
Setting a pathway through engineering and medicine
Soaring way beyond the galaxies

Becoming a best friend of law
Standing on the shoulders of proud ancestors
Regal and strength are her crowns
Making a stand of justice for all

Ronette D. Jacobs

Serendipity

A distant troop showing up for his child's typical lunch
Finding a twenty dollar bill at the gas pump
Encountering a former roommate from college

Receiving a love text from an estranged friend
Stubbing a toe on the most beautiful seashell
Discovering the perfect home while on a Sunday drive

Opening one's eyes after surgery to dear loved ones
Landing an unexpected promotion in a strained economy
Having coffee with a most cherished student from years ago

Meeting one's heart's desire while recovering
Walking into a surprise fiftieth birthday party
Opening the door to a bouquet of flowers signed "anonymous"

Hearing the voice of a best friend from childhood
Seeing the face of a former high school sweetheart
Laughing and talking on the phone for hours with a former foe

Seeing one's life portrayed across the movie screen
Connecting with a lost soul at the corner of Elm Street
Realizing life is too short to plan every moment

Leaving an antique shop richer after depositing old found coins
Rescuing a mutt which becomes the greatest friend ever
Finding destiny's path while volunteering in the community

Becoming a pro despite the meager initial triumphs
An abandoned child saving the entire estranged family
Discovering triplets when the plan was only for one

Dare to Dream

The impossibilities become the possibilities,
Seated in an audience of doubters.
You are endowed with great capabilities.
Soon you will be hunted by scouters.

The beginning has no power over the end
Dark, painful, tense, and lonely it is at times.
It only takes one right connection to mend.
Just that simple intersection makes life pleasurable.

Self-imposed limitations and barriers
Can no longer hold time in position.
For your dreams have released carriers
To help you truthfully fulfill the mission.

Accomplished solely through diligence,
Materialized by exceptions of choice,
Establishing a secure pathway for eminence,
Building one's very own distinctive voice...a dream

Courage is indeed a required attribute.
Learning from failure is a must.
Character, conscious, and conduct will contribute
To a rewarding end that is just.

For whatever has been desired in the heart
Can become a fierce reality.
A dream only requires a sincere start
In order to become a powerful finality.

Ronette D. Jacobs

Eclipsed

Eclipsed by Your unending love
Deep reflections of Your healing power
Amazed by the steadfastness of Your love
Cradled by the sweetness of grace

Resting in the kisses of Your love
Made new by the cleansing of Your blood
Wanting to drink more of You
Wrestling with time to seek more of Your face

Dancing beneath Your wings
Sheltered by the presence of Your glory
Encircled by the tenderness of You
Waiting for more gentle whispers

Echoes of love reigning over above
Revealing mysteries of a forever love
Captured by spiritual revelations
Eclipsed by Your love

Broken Chains

Modern day slave owners
Consumed by greed and blindness
Mired in selfishness and pride
Reprobated dark and webbed minds

Clinching fingers and toes
Hearts crying for freedom
Souls longing for real joy
Bodies aching for a night's rest

Visions of torment and pain
Predetermined destinies frozen in time
Unrelenting vipers of all kinds
Seeking to please their own desires

Wounded, tender, and pure
Bewildered, manipulated, and stranded
Hoping for truth to enter
Desiring to be loosed from death

Weathered by life's storms
Aware of a greater being
Fueled by a better tomorrow
Envisioning broken chains

Ronette D. Jacobs

Save Them

Let not the streets claim our daughters.
Let not the media's truth be their own.
Let not a generation be stolen forever.
Save them!

Let alcohol and drugs be aborted and not their babies.
Let education be their aim and not government aid.
Let purpose drive them and not the traps of money.
Save them!

Let not their identities be stolen or confused.
Let not the darkness be their traveling companion.
Let not wisdom and common sense be tossed aside.
Save them!

Let the sex trafficking industry be starved to death.
Let incest and molestation be strangled to death.
Let rape and suicide be sliced to death.
Save them!

Let not their hearts be poisoned by lies.
Let not their dreams be stolen by pain.
Let not their hopes be drenched in fear.
Save them!

Let their memories be pure and healed.
Let each day bring great favor and peace.
Let the sky be the limit of their possibilities.
Save them!

Let not domestic violence be a common foe.
Let not poverty seep its way into their lives.
Let not comparison be their strange guide.
Save them!

Let our daughters be protected and guided.
Let them soar with eagles and face the wind.
Let their lives be well lived and well loved.
Save them!

Ronette D. Jacobs

Visions of a Silhouette

A love gone too soon
A heartbeat swept away
Lingering teardrops

Searching through dreams
Never can it be what once was
Holding tight to the fading hope

Your decreasing love
A tomorrow not here
Widening of the shaft

Wading in wonders
Believing for more
Reaching for words

Jaws clinching in anguish
Relishing in tender tantrums
Pushing away reality

Deeply breathing
Drinking in now
Daring to perceive

A Lyric Soprano

Amazing soundness coming together
Released angels singing over us
Rhythmic beats dancing through the air

Nothing can compare to such motions
Trembling airwaves connect in strange places
Extreme highs and lows shaking rafters

Impeccable energy surging through the air
Paralyzed by such delicate ranges
Thrilled at the capacity of humans

German, Italian, French, and English
Projected from divine trained chords
Possessing regal and angelic beauty

Captivating motions displayed
Sweet grace bestowed upon others
A beginning for a tremendous end ahead

Ronette D. Jacobs

Mr. G's

A sacred world within a world
Rows of free therapy and great laughter
Serving the world's greatest and most overlooked

Metal, wooden, straight, rounded
Silver, brown, red, beige, rusted
Comfortable, semi-comfortable, uncomfortable

Magazines, newspapers, fliers, postcards
Rubbing alcohol, talcum powder, sanitizer
Booster seats, swirling chairs, tattered stools

Toddlers, tweens, teens, young adults, seasoned
Short, tall, tiny tots, stumpy, slim, in between
Wisdom, naïve, intellectual, oblivious

Daily news, sports, politics, religion, movies
Hot topics, old topics, controversial topics
Oldies but goodies, beats, ceiling shaking

Skilled, graceful, amazing, efficient
Random, familiar, strange, related
Lawyer, preacher, homeless, student

Shades of black, brown, red, grey
Straight, curly, short, long, medium
Protective shells, clippers, scissors

Empowering, uplifting, truthful
Incense, fragrances, baked goods
Talented, creative, astonishing

Looking Around

I see over there inches away
A man whose fit for life
Destined to be all he can be no matter what

Yonder, I see a woman bruised and broken by life
Seeking hope, seeking love, and seeking peace
A family torn by habitual violence

Beyond that running stream,
I see a family knitted together in love
Encompassed by wonderful memories and hopes

Above the green and lively meadows,
I see a senior forgotten by his loved ones
Set aside to die alone in a world filled with people

Around, I see love, pain, peace, and chaos
Seeking to exist in the same world
Hoping to overpower the weakest one

Even there, I see a handsome one
Sparked by the ugliness of the soul
Seeing only darkness and crying for light

Further, I see one wrenching in pain
Desiring to be free of the earthly handicaps
Knowing that a day of freedom is sure to come

Beneath, I glimpse one hoping to get beyond
Trusting in a better day than yesterday
Believing yet and still that all things are possible

Ronette D. Jacobs

America

Her beauty runs from coast to coast.
None can compare to her trails and hills.
She bares the stripes of those lives lost.

Her true history is rich in struggle and resilience.
She cannot deny her true foundation.
It is in the truth where her healing lives.

She was built upon rich red and black soil.
The sweat of generations formed the streets,
Farmed the land, and tilled the ground.

Her land is a shining wonder of the world.
She draws the world with her discoveries.
She sets the pace for others to follow.

Her God is sovereign and mighty.
She yields herself to care for others.
Her freedom empowers her people.

America, America, America!
She is a wonder to bestow.
For there is none like her.

Beyond the Four Walls

A divine and exquisite gathering place
Decked in glamour, glitz, and wonder
Packed to standing room only
An indescribable occasion
A tremendous spiritual dining moment
Beyond the four walls though,

There is a fierce hunger and thirst for your

     service.

        love.

           kindness.

              smile.

                  visit.

                      hope.

Ronette D. Jacobs

Going Home

May I soon see you again?
Traveling across the massive ocean
To place my feet upon the soil of my ancestors
To gather in a place to hear stories of your journeys
To give of my time, talents, and treasure
To rest my longing heart

Numbered Days

Seventy is the divine promise for those who believe.
A long life is promised for honoring mothers and fathers.
Healthy eating, exercising, and living assure longevity.

To some, it is rejoicing at a centennial celebration.
To many, it is breaking the mold during the golden year.
To others, it is merely blowing out sweet sixteen candles.

Man's concrete agenda holds no power over destiny.
Life span equivalency is yet a whisper and draws humility.
Putting off for that day brings great risk and falsehood.

Permanency laughs in the unseen face of what stands ahead.
Material possessions chuckle at the desires of their owners.
For another life will come, and they will belong to another.

Invincibility walks through every young life.
Immaturity attempts to hold onto youth long past its reign.
Limitability demands one find his path and give his all.

Fleeting failure may come as a lesson learned and a life lived.
Yet, regret will come as a lesson learned for a life lived in fear
For the goal must always be to seek to hear "a job well done".

Ronette D. Jacobs

Paraclete

You have been my soul's delight.
Every moment You have come in
Just in time to save my life.
Your guidance has shielded my destiny.

You have covered unmentionable moments.
For me, You have drenched my deepest wounds
In Your very precious healing balm.
What had been damaged has now become whole.

What was seen as useless has now become a jewel.
Those things unrecognizable have become clear.
With You, life has become worth living.
With You, life has become worth sharing.

Your amazing power has strengthened the weak,
Standing in total reverence to Your inner workings.
Never are the minutest details overlooked.
When You show up, nothing else matters.

When Your presence establishes order, all else fades.
Such an amazing Comforter, Guide, and Help!
Revealing longed for hopes and dreams,
Your love satisfies beyond imagination.

Your ways transforms a stony heart!
Your love sanctifies a lost soul!
Your power can never be true without You!
Life can never be fully lived without You!

Dear One

"Oh, wasn't it great?" the devil asked.
"I know you enjoyed the ride," dear one.
"I now have you where I want you to be, alone."
The fearful soul sat there and listened as Satan strolled around.
The man's eyes were full of fear, religion, pride, and unforgiveness
That had consumed his life.

"Where did I go wrong?" asked the poor soul.
"I went to church," he mumbled.
"I thought I did all the right things," he thought.
"I even wore the right color suits, and
I never missed a meeting!" he shouted.

"Ha, ha, ha," replied Satan.
"Yes, you, too, thought that was the way to heaven.
You let my words to you suck you away from the truth.
You let offenses and mistakes of your past bleed you dry.
I laid the bait and you believed…believed that it was over."

"I only wanted to see Jesus. I only wanted to go to heaven,"
the dear soul cried.

"You would have gone dear one,
if you had not taken me into your heart, and
if you had not believed the lies I told you
about yourself, others, and your future.
Now, we can spend eternity together," Satan hooted.

The man cried, "Oh, but if I had another chance…
another day to receive the Lord in my heart.
If I had but a second to receive Him, not for show,
not for what He can do, but for who He is.
Oh, but if I had another day to worship Him,
to honor Him, and to know Him, truly.
Forgive me, Oh, Lord," cried the man. "Forgive me, Oh, Lord,"
he cried as he fell to the floor.

Ronette D. Jacobs

A sudden thunder, a sudden flash!
The man awakened to himself,
sitting in the midst of praying saints.
He arose from his seat and ran to the altar,
Crying, "I surrender, Lord! I surrender!"

Immediately, God wrapped His arms around Him and said…
"I've been waiting for so long, but I am glad you came.
I am glad the saints never ceased praying for you,
For I know the plan and purpose for your life.
You, dear one, shall live and not die!
You shall accomplish all that I have foreordained for you.
I love you, dear one! Dear one, I love you, so!"

Dear Reader,

I hope that you have enjoyed your walk through *HEARTBEATS - A Journey Through the Soul.* If you would like to share how a particular poem(s) has impacted your life, I would love to hear about your journey. Thank you for investing in this promise. May your journey ahead be one filled with love, joy, peace, confidence, and great blessings.

Should you desire to share your responses, you may e-mail me at rdjheartbeats@gmail.com. Again, thank you for taking this journey with me.

To order more copies, please visit www.amazon.com. Thank you for your interest.

CPSIA information can be obtained at www.ICGtesting.com
Printed in the USA
BVOW03s2106310314

349326BV00006B/143/P